COLOUR ME GOOD CHAPPELL ROAN

THE UNOFFICIAL CHAPPELL ROAN COLOURING BOOK

Mel Elliott

Chappell Roan is a registered trademark owned by Chappell Roan. This is an unofficial, unauthorised and independent book. It does not purport to indicate trade origin connected with any of the individuals featured in this book. Neither any such individual nor anyone acting for or associated with any such individual have given their permission to publish this book or for any such individual to be included in this book. Whilst the publishers believe all statements of fact in this book to be true at the time of publishing, they do not accept any responsibility in this regard.

Chappell Roan's real name is Kayleigh Rose Amstutz. Her stage name is inspired by her late grandfather David Chappell, and his favourite song 'The Strawberry Roan'.

She is from Willard, Missouri:
The show-me state.
Here, I'll show you!

Willard has a population of just 6,000 and apparently there are more cows than there are people.

She left home and moved to Los Angeles on her own in 2018. She drove for 3 days to get there.

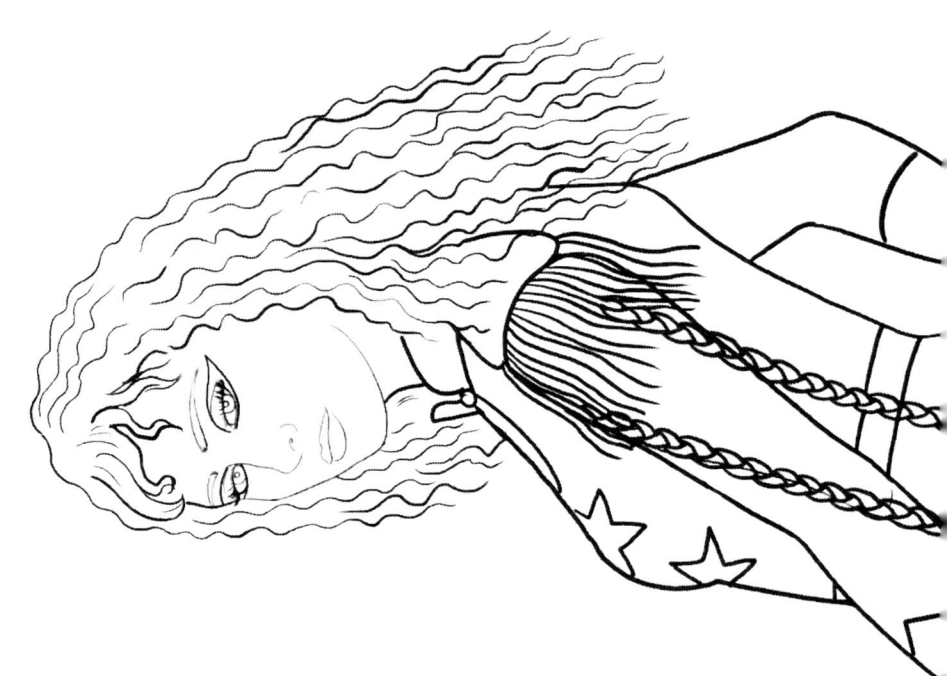

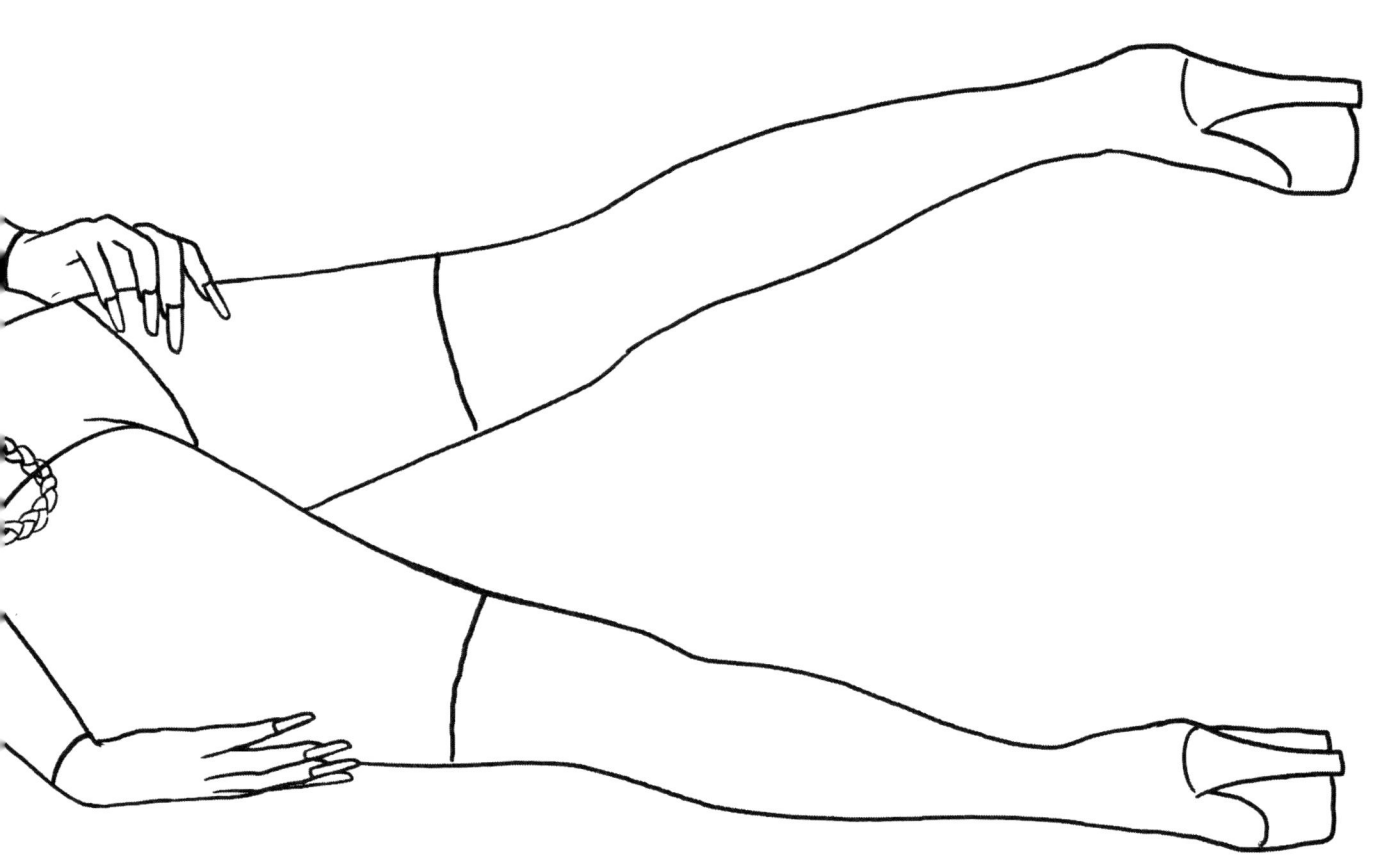

WORD SEARCH

The Rise and Fall of a Midwest Princess is Chappell Roan's smash hit album. Can you find all of its tracks in the word search?

- GOOD LUCK BABE
- RED WINE SUPERNOVA
- CASUAL
- PICTURE YOU
- KALEIDOSCOPE
- HOT TO GO
- MY KINK IS KARMA
- AFTER MIDNIGHT
- COFFEE
- PINK PONY CLUB
- FEMININOMENON
- NAKED IN MANHATTAN
- CALIFORNIA
- GUILTY PLEASURE
- SUPER GRAPHIC
- ULTRA MODERN GIRL

Please note: SUPER GRAPHIC and ULTRA MODERN GIRL are separated on the letter grid even though they are one song.

```
K A I L D Z X N A K E D I N M A N H A T T A N F L
J B Z Q U G R M D S A A M P S C U T R F L Q L U R
X O Q V B N H F U C J F T Y I G M T U G C M Q E Q
B W Z Y L X A K B W R T T T K N Q M Y M R N L V H
T V L Z G N H L X D G B N E L I K L R C G C D H O
O U L T R A M O D E R N G I R L N P X J K S U W T
P R W B I M G L D J E Q U T T M X K O S B W D O T
S B D M N S K O A V H J I T V K I S I N U K X B O
F U F R E W G B S E G D L V E P D D L S Y H Z X G
P J P G B Z Y L V Q Q T T R K H P E N I K C V M O
N I K E F Z G H P W E W Y E A F O B S I G A L P I
A B C S R O U U D C R W P D L E D K J E G P R U L
D C K T T G A P J R E W L W E M Q S Q G F H R M B
U R F W U E R N T L C A E I I I H Z Z A F G T K A
L I U L B R W A P B A S A N D N F E N A H F J J B
Y L O C K V E Y P F F K S E O I E G I D Y T Q C I
H Y E N L F N Y L H C G U S S N P N M S G M Y A B
D I L X P F T Z O F I C R U C O I N J L C C G S L
Z L C P Q X I V V U A C E P O M B M I W O W Y U I
T U P B S X Z W Q A J O W E P E C Y C O F G W A Q
G O O D L U C K B A B E R R E N T W F Y F Z N L O
F B N G H Z S F J I Z J S N P O W V S X E A Y G H
T G T J Q X A W C T G J P O M N X R T V E E E R O
F F G Y D P E N G H K D F V C A L I F O R N I A C
I R P W X X P W S P J K S A Z H U X A L E Y I P J
```

Her birthday is 19th February which makes her a Pisces. Draw what birthday gift you would like to give her.

She shares a co-writer and producer with Olivia Rodrigo. He is Dan Nigro. He has been writing with Chappell since 2020. "Three or four days into meeting her, I was convinced she was a superstar. She's incredibly articulate about what she wants out of a song and we have a great relationship when it comes to creating music" he said about Chappell.

When she is not making music, she loves to play on her Nintendo Switch. Her favourite games are The Sims, Fortnite and Mario Kart. She claims to know every cheat code on The Sims 2 "I would make everyone have twin baby aliens!" she once said.

While she was aiming for success, Chappell worked as a counsellor at a summer camp. What things are making you anxious that you would like to tell her about?

Chappell is from a very conservative area and had a religious upbringing. "I always had such a hard time being myself and felt like I'd be judged for being different or for being creative".

She is heavily inspired by drag and her favourite drag artist is Sasha Colby. When she moved to LA, she would spend time at a club called The Abbey and this inspired her song 'Pink Pony Club'. "All of a sudden I realised I could truly be any way I wanted to be, and no one would bat an eye" she says of her night at the Abbey.

Chappell was so nervous when 'Pink Pony Club' was released, thinking that it wouldn't be accepted and that people wouldn't like it.

The video was filmed in a bar, empty other than a few bikers. In the video, she nervously dances on the stage wearing tasselled and bedazzled cowboy hat and boots.

Eventually, she becomes more and more comfortable before really letting herself dance like no one is watching.

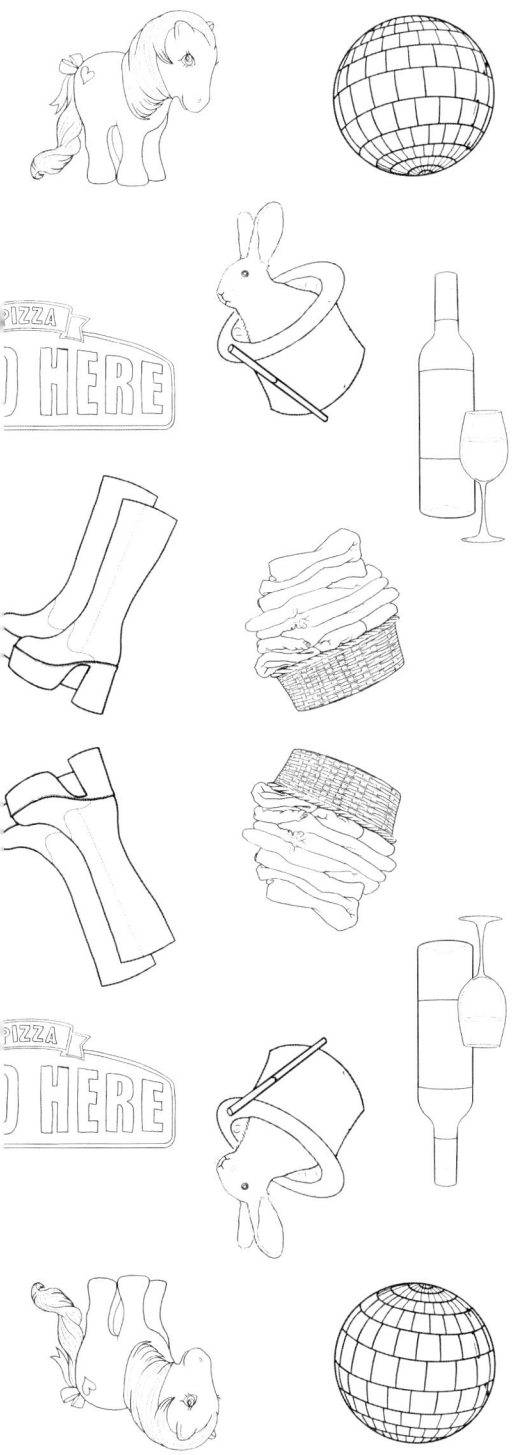

Three Chappell Roan songs are depicted in the pattern. Do you know which ones? If you don't, check out some of her lyrics!

1) ....
2) ....
3) ....

CROSSWORD

DOWN

1. She shares this producer with Olivia Rodrigo
4. Call her this not pretty!
6. Chappell's favourite shoe brand
8. Where she is from, there are more of these than there are people
10. Raise your hand now...
12. Is it _____ now?

ACROSS

2. She was born in this month
3. She is this type of princess
5. See pretty patterns revolve in this
7. Kiss this many boys in bars
9. Club that inspired Pink Pony Club
11. Town in Missouri where she is from
13. Chappell's favourite pizza company

Chappell started learning piano at the age of 12 and soon after, won a talent contest. She then began posting covers of songs onto YouTube before uploading her first original song aged 14. At the age of 17 she was signed to Atlantic. She released an EP called 'School Nights' and a single called 'Good Hurt'. She was dropped by Atlantic in 2020 when she started to change her creative direction.

Chappell's debut album, 'The Rise and Fall of a Midwest Princess' was released in 2023 but it wasn't until 2024 that it really took off and fuelled her rise to super stardom.

Chappell says that singing is what she was born to do and I'm sure you all agree!

Keep doing what you're doing Chappell, we love you!

Don't forget to follow me and show me your colouring efforts!
◉ @officialmelelliott

UK wholesale from
Turnaround UK
Rest of World wholesale available at
ilovemel.faire.com

Published by
I LOVE MEL
Printed in UK, 2024

melelliott.com
©M S Elliott 2024